MANAGEMENT FROM
HEART
—— AN OVERVIEW ——

MANAGEMENT FROM
HEART
AN OVERVIEW

ANIL KUMAR BHATIA

White Falcon
Publishing
www.whitefalconpublishing.com

Management from Heart an Overview
Anil Kumar Bhatia

www.whitefalconpublishing.com

Requests for permission should be addressed to
consultanil18566@gmail.com

ISBN - 978-1-63640-202-4

EVERYBODY IS A LEADER
THIS IS FOR EVERYBODY
and
THIS IS FOR THE LEADER

UNITING HEAD AND HEART

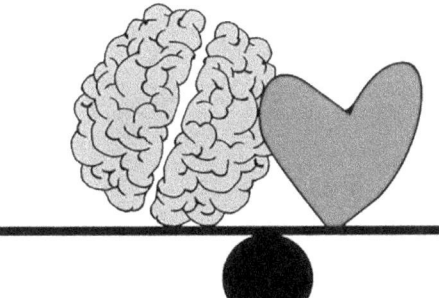

CONTENTS

PREFACE

Dear friends,

Management from the *Heart* is not a book or a biography. It is basically a bunch of feelings that I have lived through in my life. The crux of my experiences as a Manager, an Entrepreneur, a Leader, a Learner, a Follower, a Subordinate, a Junior, a Senior, a husband, a father, a brother and so on.

The golden words which came to me during my journey are

> *'MANAGEMENT IS SIMPLE BUT NOT EASY. IT REQUIRES YOUR FULL TIME AND DEDICATION. IN OUR ENDEVOUR TO MAKE IT EASY, WE COMPLICATE IT.'*

From my childhood days, I have been very fond of reading and a strong believer in the fact that we can learn a lot from other people's experiences which come to us from reading. When I started my career, after a short learning phase I was pushed by destiny into the field of MANAGEMENT, and

I felt that it was too early. Today I know that every person in this world is a Manger or, to put it in a better way – a Leader, it is GOD given. This word Leader will also be replaced by some other better word during the course of these NOTES.

My journey is largely influenced by ladies who are homemakers. I am astonished to see the skills, versatility, and management capabilities of my mother and my wife. The Indian family structure has inspired my management style and I have been able to do my job as a manager fairly successfully using these insights. I have learnt and successfully implemented a series of observations which I gathered through my family, my neighbourhood, my school, and my college through my friends and through life in general.

Management from the *heart* is a collection of notes which I have used, observed, learnt and followed during my 35-year journey as a manager. Nowadays there is a trend which tries to show that the 'leader' is more important than the 'manager'. I feel that this discussion is the same as 'idea' is more important or 'implementation'. We will talk more about this when we talk about 'who is the leader' and the 'flow of leadership'.

For me 'management' is concerned with human beings. So, my experiences are related to humans. Here I imply that it has nothing to do with concepts like data management or inventory management, etc. Business management, so far, is mostly influenced by war and sports. But business and related management is in no way related to war and sports. Business is life and has to be lived. It is not a competition and it is not an event. It is a perennial, never ending commitment. I realised that all the problems have simple solutions. Nothing comes in life easily. Management is all about widening the comfort zone of the individual team members. It is as simple as parenting. Definitely it is not easy.

A LEADER'S STATEMENT OF PURPOSE

I want to make everyone around me happy. My portfolio includes everybody -EVERYBODY.

What is happiness?

In the work field, happiness comes from -

accomplishment,

fulfilling the desired results,

achieving,

performing and smooth functioning.

My purpose is to provide an atmosphere where functioning is smooth. I try to help people fulfil their desire to be the best by providing means and methods to accomplish the best. I try to get information about what people around are doing and try to share it with everyone in my organisation. I try to provide milestones. My purpose is to show confidence in the team by appreciating and supporting them. My purpose is to make leaders who are able to build a happy and progressive atmosphere.

My purpose is to be happy. Only an organisation where in every person is happy, performs and grows.

CRISIS TO ALL-IS-WELL MANAGEMENT

I am working on an unconventional categorisation of management. On the basis of the attitude required for certain type of management I have categorized them as –

1. Crisis management
2. Change management
3. Consistency management and
4. All-is-well management

Normally I am not in the favour of categorisation as it creates distinct boundaries and impermeable walls. These walls gradually turn into silos which divide the organisation internally. But, in this case I felt it is necessary because in practice there is a lot of confusion resulting in management complications.

In the absence of clarity of this categorization we mess up between the attitudes required to handle different types. We end up playing cricket with a hockey stick.

As an example, it's my experience that 'crisis management' is much simpler than 'all-is-well management'. The team members are motivated by the situation itself while keeping the team in high spirits under 'all-is-well' situation is a very difficult ball. Crisis brings the best and all-is-well brings complacency.

Evidently both are different ball games.

The above mentioned four conditions are totally distinct and cannot be merged. If possible, in organisations, there should be different sets of people from the top to the supervision levels for managing these conditions.

A manager involved in 'crisis management' has a different mind-set as compared to someone who is managing 'all-is-well' condition. It is practically impossible for any human to switch roles between such diverse situations. The attitude and methodology of one type is quite different from that of the other.

I am not in favour of categorisation as it creates distinct boundaries and impermeable walls. These walls gradually turn into silos which divide the organisation internally –

AB-MFH

If at all it is necessary to have a common team or some common team members then the shift should be done systematically by giving a breather, classroom training, meditation sessions, and on-the-job reorientation. This is not a click change condition. The same is true for the top management also. All policy and strategic decisions right from hiring to retiring, upgrading, re-positioning, etc. should be based on the above categorisation.

There are no switchovers for this. This change needs to be done consciously and systematically.

Can you ask a javelin thrower in a competition to go and run the 100 meters dash?

Both are athletic events.

Difficult?

I never said that management is easy.

LIFE, BUSINESS, and MANAGEMENT IS NOT WAR?

Business is not war. It is not a sport either

A war is fought with enemies and a business is a process of self-improvement.

A war is destructive and a business is constructive.

A war requires demolishing the opponent and business is co-existence.

A war is normally fought with surplus resources and a business is always about optimising resources.

A war is a process of death and in business we build lives.

A war is an event.

It begins and then everyone starts searching for the end. Surely there is a beginning and an end.

Businesses are not started so that they end. Here the intention is permanence, continuity, and an endless, limitless pursuit.

I, being son of an army officer, was always fascinated by the style of the armed forces and being a sports person attracted to the systematic training approach and focused lifestyle of the players and their coaches. Then destiny pulled me into the field of business and management. Being in the field I started studying literature related to management. Soon I analysed that most of the management was influenced by war and sports.

I started practising and applying what I was learning. I was becoming successful but the concepts which I was trying to apply invariably started well, grew large and successful but faded over a period of time. There was a striking variance which I could feel. With 20 years of success as a manager I came to a point of realisation.

But almost all literature that is available deals with management keeping the concept of 'sports' or 'war' in the background. Reading it and listening to the various stories, I always had a feeling of being in or studying about the armed forces or being involved in some sort of sports and preparing or participating in some event like the National Games, the Commonwealth Games or, in case we are performing in that level, the Olympics.

The concepts of targets, deadlines, presentations, cut-throat competition, survival instincts, behaviour skills, attitude building.

The concept of management - 'Is it really related to sports or war?'

Are we at war when we are doing business?

In our daily lives, are we pursuing any sport?

In our businesses, whether it is an industry, marketing, or any other field are we able to correlate it with a war like situation?

Is our activity, in any way, identical to war?

Are we handling soldiers or dealing with enemies or dealing with guns, tanks, planes?

Are we doing business to quash our enemies?

Are there enemies out in the field and terrorists in our offices and business areas?

How are our activities related to sports or war? I simply fail to understand.

LIFE, BUSINESS, and MANAGEMENT IS NOT A SPORT?

PRACTICE IS THE KEY FOR SPORTS

In sports the main aspect is that sportspeople prepare, prepare, and prepare for an eventual day when all their practice and preparation shall fructify into a tournament. Practice is the key here. All energies are focused to prepare and keep the player ready for the 'the day'. There is a preparation gap and practice opportunity before the tournament and between two tournaments. At times, the player may not be required to perform at all.

Prepare ----- > Prepare ----- > Prepare ----- > Perform

Rest

Prepare ----- > Prepare ----- > Perform

Rest

Prepare ----- >

Is business like that in any way?

Do I give time to my team to practice and prepare in order for them to participate in my business activity for that one fine day when we will take production or one fine day when we shall go out to the market with our product?

Do I train my cashier and allow him to practice for 6 days and then on a particular day prepare bills and then practice again for next 6 days? For me, there is no practice time.

> *We should refrain from attempting to draw a workable strategy for life, business, and management from war or sports analogies*
>
> *- AB-MFH*

When in business we have to face the challenges and perform day in and day out. We don't have long practice session and long preparation periods. At best we have some opportunity to attend a few seminars, a few classroom trainings here and there, and the opportunity to 'see' or 'talk to' other senior performers. Dear friends - imagine our cricket team playing a tournament every day for two years non-stop every day. Do you expect this team to become the best team in the world? What will be the status of our players? What will be the performance of the Sachin Tendulkars and the Chris Gayles of the world?

> **In business, life, and management this is how it is**
>
> Perform - > Perform - > Perform - > - > - >Perform
> Every day.... Every time....24x7....365.25 days.... &
> .... Always.
> No practice time...Always on the field.... Hands
> always in gloves.... Pads on....

I am in no way undermining the value of our great armed forces or our sports persons. I wholeheartedly appreciate the soldiers whose sacrifices enable us to live a peaceful life. My only contention is that the philosophy which we use in the Army or the philosophy with which we train our sports people to excel is different from the philosophy on which I can work my business up. The principles have to be developed independently for business activities.

We should refrain from attempting to draw a workable strategy for life, business, and management from war or sport analogies.

BEGINNING OF THE JOURNEY

The more I thought about the variance, the more I was convinced that the theories that I was following were not going to lead me to fruition. Then there was an unknown sea in which I was swimming with no clue and no support. Now I was in a difficult situation. The dilemma was that any time I faced a situation, which we do every day, every time, my prior knowledge would guide me to do something and my new found realisation would contradict it. I was a mess. There was a resentment from within. My inner self was averse to accepting all business management systems and principles such as target, meetings, etc. I could not evolve at all.

One fine day, I went to my parental house, still contemplating (when we are upset we go to our parents). I stayed with my father and mother for a few days. Instinctively they knew that something was wrong. They showed their concern but could not contribute much mainly because I did not know what to ask. And after a few days, still without an answer and clueless, I planned to leave.

While leaving, my mother had come out to say goodbye.
Eureka!
MOTHER!!!
Yes....

*That's the answer to my quest for management principles.
My HOME is where I have to seek the solutions to all my
problems, including those of management.*

This is how the NEW journey began...

LEADERS ARE BORN

Someone asked me whether leaders are born, or can we learn to be good leaders.

Is leadership an art or a science?

Can we learn leadership skills?

I slammed,

'Leaders are not made leaders are born'.

Did my answer amaze you? ... Yes.

Leaders are born because everybody is a born leader. Leadership is as natural as parenthood because every parent is a leader. The only need is to acknowledge it.

Do we doubt our role as a father or a mother?

Do we think for a moment when guiding our children to achieve great results in high school about our capabilities as individuals?

Don't we coach our children?

Are we professionally trained coaches?

It is only a question of perception. A leader believes that he is a leader just like parents believes that they are the parents. That is the first step. Believe you are a leader – HAVE

FAITH, and you will be a leader. That's how you have been made. It is natural. You have all the hardware and software of a leader.

How do we become leaders to our children?

We, the homo sapiens, are supposed to walk on two legs. That's how nature has built us. Do we walk on two legs immediately on birth or say naturally like many other animals do? What do our parents do to make us walk on two legs?

Do all children start walking at the same age and with the same ease?

Some people start early some take a longer time. Some do it easily and some fall a several times before getting on their feet. But sooner or later every normal human being starts walking on two feet. The parents don't read manuals or dictate SOPs to a child to explain to him the art of walking. They simply encourage the child to bring out his potential.

It is the faith that I am the father or the mother. You talk to your children with that authority. You feel responsible for their actions. *That's what a leader is. He feels responsible for the actions of his followers* (children). He shares ALL of his brains with his followers. His intentions are to make the children better than himself. That makes him a great parent and a great leader. So, if you want to be a good leader simply believe that you are, and you will be.

VERY SIMPLE INDEED.

THE SPECTATOR'S VIEW

THE STORY

Master blaster Sachin Tendulkar is on the crease. Everybody in the stands and in front of TVs is praying. Sachin keep calm... keep calm.... keep calm.... The ball comes in and against the calls of millions. Those who have never held a bat in their life, mothers, wives, sisters, brothers, uncles. He goes for the big hit and is caught in the deep. Every spectator was right, and the master was wrong. This is the power of the SPECTATOR'S VIEW. You don't need to be a master just go for the spectator's view and you will get the right perspective.

Sachin, the greatest cricket star, is batting on the crease. He is at 112, playing against the arch-rivals- Pakistan. OUT! What a silly way to get out. Why did he try to nudge an outside the off-stump delivery?

He should have left it alone.

Blah blah blah.

Who is giving these expert comments?

It's me.

I have never played cricket even at the school level. AND

I am commenting.

And commenting correctly.

On the folly of the star batsman of the world.

Am I better than Sachin?

Do I know cricket more than him? NO.

I have spectator's view and he has player's view.

Yes.

That's the difference between the two of us. What he missed as a player, I realised as a spectator – *even without knowing the subject well.*

I feel this is the biggest management tool that I can offer. No other single management tool can help any leader more than this one simple tool. You get your best analysis of a situation when you put yourself in the spectator's seat and come out of player's shoes.

The irony of the situation is that you don't realise when you have shifted from being the spectator to being a player. Once you are a player you are bogged down with the limitations of the player –

I have the spectator's view and he has the player's view.

YES...

That's the difference between the two of us. What he missed as a player I realised as a spectator – even without knowing the subject well.

- AB-MFH

Probably one of the best, biggest, and the most effective tools in problem solving. We all have been told for generations – *'If you are not able to solve a mathematical problem. Leave the problem. Go to sleep. After waking up, go to the problem again and you will get the solution.' This is nothing but being temporarily in the spectator's seat; taking a wide-angle view of the problem* and utilising it to see the situation vividly to reach the solution.

INDEPENDENCE, INTERDEPENDENCE, OR COEXISTENCE?

Man has been running after INDEPENDENCE for ages. Somehow, we feel that independence is a great treasure or a great boon or something, something very aspirational and something that can transform our lives...

Various societies and civilisations have fought fierce battles for this cause – being independent.

What is INDEPENDENCE?

Defined (Cambridge dictionary)

'The ability to live your life without being helped or influenced by other people.'

So, if I take the above definition,

Is this state possible in this universe?

Is this natural?

Can we get one example of independent existence of any LIVING being in nature?

NO. An impossible state!

That's nature – COEXISTENCE.

So, the conclusion is that by trying to be independent we are attempting the impossible. We are seeking something unnatural. To smoothen the jerk let's start with a softer word – more independence. Parents are advised to give their children more independence. Sounds better.

Nature is a combination of highly interdependent existences who cannot thrive without each other. These existences are continuously providing and receiving sustenance materials from each other.

To exist together, at the same time, or in the same place.

To live in peace with another or others despite differences, especially as a matter of policy.

YES.

A realistic combination of independence and interdependence is called **coexistence**. *And that is a real-life term. All our management principles have to understand the basic concepts of coexistence to be practical. We have to deal with the challenges of coexistence and take advantage of the benefits of coexistence.*

We coexist with people who are similar, opposite, and indifferent.

We have to face the basic attributes of it like an intra-species competition and an inter-species competition. We have to consider predators as well. We have to regard the natural laws like the survival of the fittest, the big fish eating the small fish, the survival niche, competitive exclusion, and so on.

Now management is more natural.

HAPPINESS LIES IN SUCCESS

DO WHAT YOU ARE SUCCESSFUL IN

My experience is in contradiction to modern thinking which advertises
'do what you like'.
The better version could be
'do what you are successful in'.

Most of the biographies and autobiographies that I have gone through reveal that the person was doing a work or following a career which was at odds with his choice. All those great people, which I read had this common denominator – they pursued something which was not what they wanted to do. They were pushed into something by chance, then they realised that they are getting successful and continued.

But they were all invariably happy because they were successful.

If I wanted to be a painter and was not able to transfer my thoughts to the canvas, would I be happy?

I took courses in painting but still I did not have a knack for it.

No one and including myself could appreciate my creations. Could pursuing that field give me happiness or bitterness?

Instead, I became an engineer who was able to become a good and successful manager.

From the word go I was successful in this field.

I could grow, explore, contribute and so I was and am happy.

MAKE THEIR SUCCESS

If you want people to be happy show and acknowledge their success.

Better is to 'make their success'.

What I like to do but am not able to do well does not make me happy or satisfied. What I do successfully makes me happy and satisfied. Stop thinking about what makes me happy and satisfied. Stop thinking what you like and start doing what you are successful in. You will be happy and satisfied. That's the crux of perspectives after reading a number of autobiographies, biographies, and also that of my life.

If the life of your choice doesn't bring in the corresponding success you envisaged it to bring in, it could be discouraging. In fact, I would not suggest to anyone to follow their hobbies or interests into their profession unless they are 7(+)/ 10 on them . If it is less, it may be more satisfying to do something in which you can be successful.

I always say, *'Comfort is the largest and fastest selling commodity'*.

But something bigger than this motivates people to do great jobs like scaling peaks, competitive events, entrepreneurship, etc. This something extra is steered by the feelings of success. Motivation for this definitely comes from within but leaders do have a big role here.

SUCCESS DEMONSTRATED

If a leader is able to demonstrate to his followers that the path on which they are moving will lead to success he will have a motivated team. Very simple. As a team leader we have to show small successes in the direction of the bigger ones. This not only keeps the team engaged, it also helps in keeping them together and in high spirits.

Nothing succeeds like success – create small successes.

A KING WITHOUT
HIS OWN EYES

Rishi Vyas created the *Mahabharata*. It is about how the EGO of a blind king led to the war of the Mahabharat which changed the course of this world. This included the avatars of Vishnu, Shree Krishn, the Pandavas and the Kauravas.

> *'The king should never be blind. He has to use his own eyes to see the situation...'*
>
> *- AB-MFH*

In his creation, Rishi Vyas has explained the personality of each character involved. He has given vivid descriptions of all the characters. Each character represented some special trait which ultimately affected the final outcome - the Mahabharat. There was one character, the most important character, who was the real basis of the Mahabharat - Dhritrashtra, the king. The blind king. Dhritrashtra was the elder brother of Pandu but because of being blind, he did not get the kingdom. The untimely death of Pandu forced the system to make him the king. Here Rishi Vyas has clearly depicted the importance of the physical fitness of the king.

Why did Rishi Vyas portray Dhritrashtra to be blind?

This is the only blind character in whole epic. A 'blind king' is the root cause of...

It's one of the biggest lessons I feel Rishi Vyas communicated through this character - 'The king should never be blind. He has to use his own eyes to see the situation.'

If you are a decision-maker, please keep your EYES open. Toyota system, probably, explains the same when they use 'Gemba' - visit and see the actual place where value is created.

A beautiful example of same concept also comes in the *Ramayana*. When after coming back to Ayodhya and settling as the king of Ayodhya Shree Ram was told by his informers about the unrest in the common people about Queen Sita, he did not take it blindly. In fact, Shree Ram felt that the informer was not giving the complete picture and so he decided to go out in disguise to get the real picture.

We can find many incidents in life of great entrepreneurs like Henry Ford, Jamshedji Tata, Ratan Tata, etc. where we can feel that they were personally and directly connected to the field of work.

This is vital.

Video conferencing is more popular and practical than an audio concall

The head or the main decision maker cannot be blind. He has to use both his faculties to gage the information, ears and eyes. Reading data, design, and details is also the crucial role of the eyes. The ears are also equally important to receive information from all 'related' members. I have also remarked that video conferencing is more popular than audio concalls (which have been available for quite some time) because people communicate more visually than only through words.

WE ARE TRAINED WRESTLERS PLAYING FOOTBALL

WRESTLING IS -

A one-man sport.

The competitor is the enemy - and the aim is to demolish the opponent.

The team member is also a competitor - as two players from same team can also compete and are definitely competing during practice.

Train for self – every person is training to improve his power and skills.

Win for self – the victory is of the person first. The winner's first recognition is his name followed by the team.

Positional – the categories are based primarily on the body weight of the player himself.

FOOTBALL IS -

A team sport.

Competitor is the enemy – the aim is not to physically harm the enemy.

The team member are supporters and co-players – you have to first be a good team player to be a successful football player.

Trainings with team – you have to practice and train with the team. Even if you are practising striking still you need your goalkeeper friend. It is a game of coordination and 'co-operation'.

Win for team – the victory is of the team.

Relational – the whole process is relational. Even the field placements are relational. The players try to complement each other.

> *From the time we are born we are trained to be wrestlers, an individual sport. From kindergarten to primary to college... We are always being trained as a wrestler and in our organisations, we are expected to play football, a team game. Let all leaders be aware of this.*

PERCEPTION OR TRUTH?

At times I tell my two team members who are in conflict - it is all about perception; you may be true as per your perception and the other may be true based on his or her perception.

I remember a childhood story of six blind men describing an elephant. One says it is like a fan, another compares it to a rope, another says it's like a pillar...

There is also another picture of a cylinder whose shadow appears round from one light source and rectangular from another.

In life, business, and management we are dealing with humans who have all the senses and today even extended senses. We are not fixed sources of light. We can move and verify – it is cylindrical. The issue is the rigidity of our stance and not the perception. Perceptions do change if we are flexible enough.

Is it a conflict situation which we are trying to avoid behind perception?

In business we should talk on facts. If one person says it is 6 and another 9, we cannot say both are correct. The truth is one – either 6 or 9.

Business or management decisions cannot be based on perception and the argument that two people can have different perceptions does not hold good. We can verify the perceptions and find the truth which may be a third angle. *Truth is important not the perception.* Perception is verifiable by opening our eyes, entering the other person's shoes and using the required tools.

Let us stop hiding behind perceptions and face the truth.

DE-BOTTLENECKING, EXPANSION AND TRUST

How can any business sustain itself?
The only way is growth.
How can a business grow?
There are only two ways:
De-bottlenecking and expansion and both have to go simultaneously hand in hand.

(A) DE-BOTTLENECKING – Any job, activity, or process consists of a number of steps. Identifying these steps and finding the bottlenecks and clearing them. This is a continuous never-ending process for improvement.

(B) EXPANSION – Reinvesting on expansion and growth is mandatory for the survival. It may be integration or diversification, but without expansion sustainability is not possible.

Expansion is normally easy to understand and is luring as the results are easily visualised.

De-bottlenecking is much more vital. It is more difficult too as it needs introspection. Introspection is one of the most difficult jobs.

A little review of all great businesses around us will easily reveal this aspect. It is continuously finding its weak zone and converting it into a strong area. Now some other zone will be comparatively weaker waiting to be strengthened...

A CASE

How have many successful businesses grown?

A friend of mine started a small business in a garage and today he has a multinational presence. Today also he, through his team, is continuously working on de-bottlenecking the individual entities and expanding with new developments. On the other hand, those who started with wonderful products but did not accept the existence of bottlenecks and avoided expansion are not visible at all. They are only remembered in business management classes.

The third and the most important factor is TRUST. The importance of this factor makes it necessary to be dealt with separately.

MANAGING WITHOUT TARGETS THE STORY

A few years back I joined an organisation as their HOD (Head of Operations). Before my formal interview, I was given a review of their existing facilities and a tour of the factory. In the interview, the board members asked me about my estimation of their capacity of production. Unaware of what their actual production levels are, based on my experience and calculations, I gave a figure of 80 units per day. After a good interview, I was selected and I joined the group. On joining, a senior board member called me and told that we are making 30 units per day. He also told me that I should plan in such a way that we produce 900 units per month because that is what we can sell. After 3 years with them we were at 80 units per day with 2200 to 2400 units per month. But 2 years after that we were stuck at the same level.

There are two distinct periods –

First 3 years –

30 - > 35 - > 50... - > 60 - > 65... - > 70 - > 75 - - - > 80

we worked on de-bottlenecking. The whole team was involved in finding the weak links and making necessary strengthening arrangements. From 30 to 35 to 50 to 55....80. Wow! We were making 2200 units and selling them too. From we cannot sell more than 900 to actually selling 2200 units every month. All this without any target.

In the next 2 years – we expanded, added more equipment, more capacity. But still we were 2200 to 2400. We had a capacity of 120 units. Forget it! We are capable of 2200 only. During the first period the figure of 800 had become a target and now we stopped our de-bottlenecking process. No, we cannot go beyond 2400, 2200 is good enough! An un-visualisable stagnation and satisfaction creeped in.

Today I am not with them but still after many years with a capability of 3500 units the factory and all its workers are happy with 2200. 2400 still remains the TARGET.

Can you conceive an organisation without targets?

In today's world where we also target the steps, we take in our morning walk, it is very difficult to even imagine running an organisation without targets. Very difficult. I never said that management was easy...

Every old worker is always found remembering those 3 years. In those 3 years, we cleared all the bottlenecks to reach this zenith.

A child does not study hard to score good marks in this examination, he studies hard to make his life good.

Visions should never be obscured by petty targets and targets are always petty.

You can always achieve better than the best target that you fix.

Vision needs to be fuelled by imagination and 'fiction'. It should not be restricted by history, knowledge, and an understanding of the boundaries of the organisation. Boundaries are boundless.

Can you conceive an organisation without targets?

In today's world where we also target the steps we take in our morning walk; it is very difficult to even imagine running an organisation without targets. Very difficult. I never said that management was easy...

A Target is a –	
Growth deterrent,	
Thinking restrictor,	*Synonyms for Target are*
Waste generator,	*mark, prey, and victim.*
Individualistic,	
Limiting, Insensitive.	

A TARGET is defined as –
...a person, object, or place selected as the aim of an attack.
...something that you are trying to do or achieve.
...a mark to shoot at.
...a goal to be achieved.

Cricket – I have been watching cricket for more than 35 years. During my journey of life with cricket it took almost 20 years for the players to break the mental barrier of a century (100 runs). I have seen the best batsmen quiver at 90s innumerable times. I have seen matches being lost because the star, well set player, getting out playing a stupid shot soon after crossing 100.

A century (100) is just a number and nothing but a PERSONAL TARGET. It creates so much over-focus that you tend to lose the very purpose of your existence.

Life is continuity. A series of growth steps big and small. The prospects and potential are limitless. Putting restrictions limits the horizons and so the possibility of expansion.

TARGETS ARE UNREALISTICALLY LIMITING

In the 70s, when I was in school, we were using 100watt incandescent lamps (bulbs).

If I was to give a TARGET for energy saving at that time, what would be my best, guess?

WOW – TARGET 7% PA.

My brains would be shut on minor changes, controlling losses, reducing wastage, etc. These steps don't need TARGETS, these have to be done obviously.

Only the quest for improvement and thinking differently gave us the 60 watt and 40-watt tube lights. No TARGET setter could set the 60% improvement mark. But things did not stop there. We went on to make 20-watt CFLs and 8- watt LEDs. Was it possible by setting TARGETS?

I have to go to Delhi - 300 kms. In India, the target is 5 hours. In some countries, it may be 2 hours, but can you put a target of 10 minutes or less. But despite our lives being full of such examples we see them as seemingly unachievable.

First, we set low targets and then we are content with 90% achievement. Targets are limiting and retarding. Our mindset has been such that we appreciate a person who keeps low target (90%) and achieves (89%) with difficulty over a person who keeps high target (125%) and under achieves (101%).

And 500% or 5000%? We want insane results from sane people...

THE STORY

Targets are personal not of the organisation.

When my son was in school, I told him that he should get good grades in order to be able to get admission to college of his choice. For a good life. To earn respect and reputation...

Did I tell him that his good grades will increase the turnover of the family?

It will boost the family's reputation.

Or that the family income will increase...

If I had told him that you get good grades and then you can go and beg on the streets?

Would he put all his efforts then?

'He has to put in his best for HIS future, his life'
that's what we all show our children.

What is a team member going to get if the organisation reaches level X? The clearer it is the better we can expect and many good organisations, at times unknowingly, do it. This converts the organisation's target into my target.

TARGETS ARE ENERGY DRAINERS

To achieve something big, we need maximum energy boosters and to shun energy drainers. Work is the biggest energy booster if our leader can show incremental success. Tension is the biggest energy drainer.

So, a target is a drainer as it creates tension.

TARGETS LEAD TO EXPENSIVE COMPROMISES

On a TV show there is a competition for baking cakes. A rack of utensils, cooking systems, rack of ingredients, and whatever is required for the job. A time limit of 40 minutes.

I was surprised to see that most of the time the contestant who was focussing on time ended up losing because of either -

making some irreparable error or
by not being able to complete the task in time.

Mostly (I am saying only to console myself) the contestants making moderate and just-a-cake won the competition.

Those who were making excellent cakes were also not able to finish in time. The best-to-be products usually got messed up during last few minutes under pressure of time.

The winners usually compromised on quality, finesse, and the required details.

What do you want?

A moderate product, expensive irreparable errors, tension, and compromises.

Are you looking for a genuinely good product and a happy and balanced team which is energetic?
A well finished task. Repeatable performance.

WHEN ARE TARGETS USEFUL/PRODUCTIVE?

* When the duration of event is very short, and all parameters are fully under control (still there are 4% chances of error).
* When you are in sports like situation – you have time and resources to practice.
* *When time is the only important criteria.*
* *When mediocre results are acceptable.*
* *It is a do-or-die situation and you are ready to accept the cost of death.*
* *When the leader has more important tasks than this one then it can be used as a proxy with delegation.*
* *When you are externally compelled, to catch a flight.*

ELSE

We can work without targets and we have been doing so on many occasions. **If we introspect, we can find many incidents when we achieved wonderful, more than expected results without targets -**

* We can decide the 'why' we want to do it.
* Fix a 'what' we want to achieve.
* Make guidelines of 'how'.

And do our best.

*   *Follow by logical supervision.*
*   *Empower.*
*   *Use simple human logic.*

This requires an active leadership. The leader cannot be lethargic at all. He has to be energetic and involved. Targets are for the easy-going leader who does not wish to involve himself and is happy to achieve 'X' with difficulty and who wants to shift HIS responsibility and put it on the TARGET.

Like management, target fixing is simple but not easy.

> *We can always achieve better than our best conceivable targets and targets do not allow us to achieve our best...*
>
> *AB-MFH*

WHICH CLASS IS MY CHILD IN?

IN WHICH CLASS IS MY CHILD?

'I want a teacher for my child.'

'What class?'

'My child knows nothing at all.'

The next day a lady came to my house who was a specialist kindergarten educator. She started screaming when she saw my kid.

'I want a teacher for my child.'

'What class?'

'My child knows everything that a school or college teacher can teach'.

Next day I saw Mr Sharma, the post graduate professor at my door. He went shouting when he saw my kid.

'I want a teacher for my child.'

'What class?'

'My child knows all that a school can teach.'

Next day Mr Ghosh, a college professor...

He was furious when he saw my kid.

'Strange. You are not able to arrange one teacher for my child!'

'Do you know which class your child is in?'

> *Well, this I have seen happen more than often even in organised organisations. Our own assessments about our own teams are so misleading that we end up hiring the wrong person for...?*
>
> *Self-assessment is never easy...*

MULTITASKING –
I LEARNT IN
MY SCHOOL

Yesterday my assistant came and said, 'I want to learn multitasking. Is there any course?'

'But you have already done a very long course on multitasking,' was my response.

He was surprised.

Yes.

Every one of us is well 'trained' in this. Each one of us has been taught this for days, months, and years. When we were in school and college, we had separate periods, books and notebooks, and teachers for different subjects.

From 9:00 to 9:45 we were studying maths and from 9:45 to 10:30 was time for history.

At 9:45 everything changed. We kept the maths books and notebooks in the bag and out came those for history. The moment next teacher cleared the board everything, every thought of maths vanished and we were in history. Almost 15 to 16 years of our lives we have been trained for this.

Multitasking implies doing several tasks at a time but not together, one after another without confusion. It never implies doing them simultaneously.

Simple but not easy.

Have a different set of notebooks and books.

Have a period bell between two classes.

Close the books and notebooks and clear the board.

The next class begins.

It is very simple but not easy. Remember your school days. We all were great multitaskers!

And we all are.

LEARNING TO BE A LEADER

How do I prepare myself to be a good and effective leader?

What course should I undertake to be an efficient leader?

Where do I learn leadership skills from?

PRACTICE....

Where?

Wherever you are.

My Leadership course is very simple –

Be a good child – learn from parents, teachers, and everybody around. Develop positive communication skills.

Be a good parent – develop a happy co-existence with your spouse. Learn to share your mind with your spouse. Develop positive communication skills.

Be a good neighbour – co-existence and co-development of self and neighbours. Learn to share your mind with your neighbours. Develop positive communication skills.

Be a good support to your children – develop virtual leadership level with your children. Learn to share your mind. Develop positive communication skills.

You are ready. You have learnt managing yourself with seniors, peers, colleagues, and subordinates. Rest will follow, you are a great leader. This is the greatest management school. Your seat is always reserved, only you have to make up your mind to START the learning process. Unless you are able to clear the above papers, you are sure to be a failure as a leader or entrepreneur or manager...

You are a leader - crash course in leadership the practical way.

BUILDING ATTITUDE

THE STORY

Right now, when I am writing this note there is someone inside me, my Mr Inside, who is continuously chattering. He always keeps on saying something, something, something non-stop. Yesterday my friend was telling about an incident with full enthusiasm and this Mr Inside was shouting 'bore, bore, bore...' I was almost yawning.

I was going to fire a subordinate and this fellow was yelling 'no, no, don't do that...' and I didn't.

Around 15 years back, I discovered something phenomenal. *My Mr Inside changed his dialogues when I asked him to do so.* I had to follow up with him with reminders and logic, but he obeyed for sure. Then there was another wonderful discovery. I was upset with the behaviour of a subordinate, Rameshji, although he was a very efficient and hard-working person. Every time, when Rameshji came to me this Mr Inside used to shout many negative slogans. I had a poor, indifferent attitude towards him and all our team members knew it. While having my evening tea one day I told this shouting idiot, 'Look Rameshji is a good person, a smart worker good for the organisation. You should not speak like this about him.' Next time when Rameshji was in front of me my Mr Inside was shouting praises for him.

Yes!

And my attitude towards Rameshji changed almost instantly. To control my attitude towards people and incidents I always take help of this chatterbox, my Mr Inside. You can also take help from your Mr Inside, it is a simple and effective attitude modulator, but not easy.

THE THREE TIME WASTERS

THE STORY

The other day a friend of mine told me that our Prime Minister Modiji works for 18 hrs a day. We should take inspiration from him. I don't know what inspiration my friend took but I really got a shock of my life. If Modiji is managing a country of 1350 million in 18 hrs then I should be able to manage my affairs in???

Possibly a few minutes per day.

ANALYSISNG MY TIME

I started analysing my time management which revealed following startling facts about my time wasters. In a very short time, I was able to identify and analyse my three time wasters.

THE THREE TIME WASTERS

1. WAITING -
    I did not have a plan as to how I was going to utilise my waiting times. Waiting is bound to happen and it eats away almost 40% of available time.

I asked my assistant to search google for… He is searching and I am waiting.

We have a VC at 3 PM and I am waiting 2 PM onwards.

Sometimes the waiting is for few minutes sometimes for hours. I am waiting for flight at the airport or waiting for an inspector or an auditor or some visitor, guest, vendor, customer, internal meeting.

Do I have a plan to utilize this 5min, 10 min… X hrs slots? Yes. Now I read all my emails during these waiting periods.

2. **CHOWKIDARI (THE WATCHMAN) -**

This is a very important part of our jobs, but we give it around **90 times** more than the required time. Watching what is happening is a very important task but do I give it the required time, or more, or less. In my case, I found that I was giving it 90 times more time. *The observation that I can now do in 5 mins what was earlier taking 45 mins with unnecessary garbage collection extra.*

3. **PRETENDING -**

It takes 'n x n x n x n' time, always. *Pretending to be busy not to others but to myself also. We believe important people are busy people. If I show that I am busy everyone, including myself, will feel that I am important.*

Take care of your time wasters.

I could save around 85% of my busy day and now I have plenty of time to do a lot more constructive and essential work –the real management work– learning and training.

I WANT TO SEE
THE FUTURE
THROUGH MEETINGS

Meeting is one of the most powerful tools in life, business, and management. It is an opportunity to think collectively through more than one brain and a number of hearts.

> *Meeting is a platform for transforming "ME" to "WE"*
> *- AB-MFH*

Any management tool or system which promotes communication is a good and worthy asset. Like any other tool or system, it all depends on how we use it. The same meetings which were born to increase communication and improve speedier decision-making have the potential to kill both the objectives. This largely depends on the implementor. The selection of the members and the meeting management skills of the head play a crucial role in deciding the direction of the meeting. The issue which I want to address here is that the *meetings should only be used for seeing and visualising the future*. This tool is not for post-mortems or re post-mortems. A platform which brings a number of brains and hearts together also brings a number of attitudes and EGOs.

It is an information gathering and giving mechanism but should be used very carefully as a decision-making place. The participant selection is the key. An information gathering meeting can have many related, less related, or unrelated participants but when the meeting shifts to the decision-making stage the participants should be reduced to only the direct stake holders.

A meeting is not a platform for responsibility sharing...

DON'T APPRECIATE IF...

THE STORY

A subordinate came to me excited and said, 'Eureka I have done it!'

'Wow, fantastic!'

He went away smiling. The next time when I crossed him in the corridor, he was indifferent. Actually, I had tried to pretend being excited and appreciative, but my inner voice was saying, 'Then what. This is nothing. This is what you are paid for.' I had read somewhere that we should appreciate the efforts of our team players, be an encourager, so I was acting...

Those authors, now am sure, meant that *'see the good, feel the good, and then appreciate the good'. They would have never meant that you act like an appreciator.* Even on screen only those actors are successful who really are able to enter the shoes of the character.

THE SECOND STORY

A few days back in a party that I was attending, there was a couple with their three-year-old kid. The baby was the centre of attraction in the party. Everyone, especially the ladies, were around that baby. The kid was friendly to all. Anybody was picking him, and he was giggling and playing with everybody. Mrs Neeta was standing nearby, unnoticed till someone thrust the baby into her laps. Suddenly the baby started crying and would not stop till someone else lifted him. Again, the frolic continued.

Somehow, I was not able to digest the happening. I called my wife to a side and asked about Mrs Neeta, a difficult situation normally, but my wife somehow understood that it was normal. She told me that she was a weird character. Not very friendly type. Always complaining and a real nasty one. How could a three-year-old kid sense that just by being in her lap for a few seconds? This observation led me into more practical investigation, and I found that it is not unusual. Kids are always comfortable with a few people and uncomfortable with others, even if the other person tries hard to exhibit warmth.

Is it not true with us grown up kids?

Yes, it is.

In business and management, it is normally the other way around, and that is more devastating. We know the person has done a great job. At times even better than my expectations, but... we won't appreciate. I will pretend as if it was ordinary. I am afraid to appreciate. Maybe, I am afraid because I feel that if I appreciate, he will ask for something disproportionately big. Or, if I appreciate one person, others will also start expecting.

I have many illogical reasons for not being appreciative. Ultimately, I become a PHONY and people don't like a phony. Be simple, be real, be appreciative. Appreciate as much as you feel.

Simple but not easy.

WHO IS
THE LEADER?

MFH believes that the leader is the person who is in the charge of the job. He is the head person who is really responsible for the show and he is himself able to exhibit the 'how' of the job.

When I ask this question in any organisation, I get answers like the owner, the MD, the CEO, the General manager.

THE STORY

In an organisation making bakery products I asked the owner, Mr Sharma, if he was one of the best bakers? He replied that he had never baked anything. He was an ex-army officer. He had a team of good bakers with Mr Akash as their head and Mr Akash was a brilliant baker and manager.

Then, who is the leader?

Then what is the role of Mr Sharma?

He is the resource provider.

He has to ensure that Mr Akash gets proper resources to perform including the team, material, machinery, equipment, consumables, methods, training, and education for Mr Akash and the whole team.

That is true for all organisations. *The first person who is getting a job done by a group of persons is the 'leader'.* All his team subordinates are his followers. He has his set of 'helping and supporting' peers and senior 'resource providers' to perform. **Leadership is not a post. It can flow from any person to any person, even to an outsider, or to a remotely located person.**

Leadership is flowing (to be dealt separately) but this person, Mr Akash, is most often 'the executor leader' or 'the task owner'. He is responsible for the task at hand and he is directly in command of the team and resources. He is also supposed to ensure the necessary flow of the leadership. Normally, no one above this (so called) person can really undo what is done. He has to be the real authority. The organisation head or other senior members are only supposed to review, revise, and provide.

Mr Akash directly impacts the mood, the feelings, the enthusiasm, the dedication, and the belongingness of the total group. To perform and to give the real output it is the responsibility of Mr Sharma to be the best possible provider and handover the leadership and task ownership.

But I thought that I am the leader.

CHAOS OR ORDER?
DISTANCE DECIDES.

THE STORY

I was going to the Delhi airport in a cab. I felt that I will miss the flight. I was anxious. On the way I felt that the traffic was chaotic. It appeared that there was a total lack of order and discipline. It appeared that people were just rushing here and there. It was a total disorder and randomness appeared to be at its peak. I felt that I will never make it to the airport on time, but the cab driver was cool and composed, and finally we reached, just in time. Honks and brakes... a chaos.

I reached the airport and took my flight. Now, I am in the comfort of my window seat, looking from the window of the plane. The same roads which I had just waded through, appeared beautifully ordered. The lights moving one after the other in beautiful synchronisation. A stream of lights moving in one direction and another stream in the opposite direction. The flock of lights moving together, then stopping suddenly as if they have been orchestrated.

Everything now appeared to be in order, in harmony. No chaos.

I feel that this is a good test that we can use in life, business, and management. Many a times, some things which appear to be chaotic are not really so. It may be that our point of view and frame of mind are not correct. We may be too close, too involved, too anxious that we are unable to visualise the order, the coordination, and the harmony.

> *It is always better to move a little distance away and take the calm, distant, preferably aerial view where you can see more threads and links. Then the decision of chaos or order is more relevant and real.*

THE CONFLICT – 'WHAT THE ORGANISATION NEEDS' V/s 'WHAT I LIKE'

Many activities happen in my organisation because I like them and not because the organisation needs them. The head is responsible to constantly keep this check in his mind. This contradiction normally leads to waste generation and conflict. All activities need to be directed towards the needs of the organisation both short and long term, and nothing else. Personifying 'the organisation' helps in achieving this. Law also holds the company as an identity. As I told in the discussion on the soul of the organisation, we can also have a chair for the organisation.

The most obvious example is while taking interviews for new recruitment. The organisation needs a horse and I am impressed by the mahout (the elephant rider). The temptation results in wrong hiring and a series of future problems.

Another example is that of making the team members take up a project which is not required by the organisation, but because I simply like it. Most of the time the team members either know from the beginning or get to know in due course of time but can't resist me and my logic.

This type of activity is both financially and psychologically draining and often leads to disrespect.

> *'All activities need to be directed towards the needs of the organisation both short and long term, and nothing else. Personifying "the organisation" helps in achieving this.'* - AB-MFH

At times, the need of the hour is to stay put, but I like action. I know it was a lifetime learning for me which I learned the hard way. A very difficult situation but it often comes up.

Dynamism does not necessarily mean always running, on your toes, it also involves recuperating, preparing, and waiting patiently for the right time. Unfortunately, Gen X wrongly tends to calculate efficiency by the number of hours and not by the outcome.

This is a difficult situation 'I like it' but the organisation does not 'need' it.

Management is simple but not easy.

OUT OF THE COMFORT ZONE

THE GARDEN OF EDEN –

Adam and Eve, the first humans tasted the apple and were thrown out of the Garden of Eden. They came to the world because they had tasted the apple, 'the fruit of knowledge' and so they could not then live in the 'garden of comfort'.

That is human nature. When we taste the fruit of knowledge, we are out of our comfort zones and we become seekers...

In the field of business, we have to be sure what we expect from people.

What is their JOB?

Do we require sheep work, horse work, or elephant work?

Each type of work has its own requirements. If I am in a business which requires creativity and innovation my requirement is different and if I am into a *routine activity job where the output is proportional to the time spent*, then my requirements are different. For the first case, I need to have an out of comfort zone people who thrive on being out-of-comfort zone, like Adam and Eve. On the other hand, if it is routine activity task, I have to provide a comfort-zone like atmosphere for best productivity.

This analysis shows that the production, sales, accounts, security teams should have comfortable working zones whereas marketing, research and development, design, creative teams should have out-of-comfort working zones.

But we have been thinking otherwise!

LEARNING FROM MISTAKES

'You only learn how to make mistakes from your mistakes.'
False.

THE STORY

Consider a boy who wants to be a shooter. He goes to the target, takes hold of the gun and shoots 100 fires. Today is his first day on the field. Maybe, a few shots landed on the target board. After one year the same boy reaches state level championship. He committed mistakes, maybe 95 out of 100 were mistakes, but still he corrected and today he is world champion. *Practice reduces mistakes; it is in-born in our system.* The brain is able to distinguish between failures and successes. It propels us towards more success and away from failures. That's how all successful people have worked and achieved what they wanted; it is no rocket science.

The base line is that don't worry about committing mistakes. Learn from them. The most important thing here is the coach and the confidant.

> *Learn with a confidant and commit mistakes in front of your coach. Surrender to their feedbacks and rehearse mentally. Then learning from mistakes is faster and less painful.*

Learning from mistakes - prerequisites

1. Attitude of learning
2. Acceptance of mistakes
3. Courage to face them
4. Willingness to improve and
5. Willingness to seek guidance.

For guidance one needs awareness of lack of competence. Accepting help is also an important part of the path of correction... Very true. Sometimes your ego does not allow you to take help and failures become inevitable. That is why awareness of our competence is important.

Moreover, *believe that people always love to help.* This more than sufficient reason to seek help and to learn from mistakes.

GRAB THE FIRST OPPORTUNITY

First of all, I would clarify that opportunity is not what is available every day or every now and then. Opportunity is something that comes occasionally and rarely.

THE STORY

While moving on the road in my car I saw a person selling lemon juice and felt like having one. Since I was moving at a high speed and the stall was on the other side of the road, I avoided turning back –
'The driver's EGO'.
I thought there will be more on the way and I will stop at the next one.
Zoom I passed the next one.
I will definitely stop at the next.
Next never came and I reached home.
Thirsty!
To grab an opportunity should we not be a bit more flexible.
Rigidity and EGO...

Has it yielded anything good to me or to anybody for that matter?

A small flexibility to stop and turn around could help me enjoy the lemonade and quench my thirst.

The same happens with opportunities. We are likely to miss them on our first contact. Then our EGO and rigidity stops us from turning back and grabbing it. We convince ourselves that more will come, and I will grab it now, first-hand.

Woosh... gone.

Next.

Gone.

At the first instance,

Leave EGO.

Turn back.

GRAB!

WOW!

THE DATA OVERDOSE
REDUCE TENSION
IMPROVE
PRODUCTIVITY

'Work energises and tension tires'.
Nowadays it is very common to work for extended hours, pressure of deadlines, tension to meet the targets.

I have a feeling that 'work' has reduced and 'tension' has increased. The Executors and the Doers are more tired and less efficient.

Who is responsible?
Who has to take corrective actions?
It all starts from the 'Top'.

I have seen that over a period, organisations big or small, have added a lot of 'time wasters' to their systems and the process is still on. We are trying to collect much more data, information, so-called-knowledge (unnecessary junk), etc. in the name of competition and growth.

> *We are fascinated by big cupboards having apparels which we are never going to use.*

It's high time when organisations, starting from the top, need to do some digging, analysis, and re-thinking.

We have to

- Do 'festival cleaning' of our minds and
- Stop garbage collection.

It's time to ask, 'Does my organisation really need it'. Availability of fancy items in the shop, on the rack, does not imply that I should get it, or I really need it. The 'managements' get lured by the marketeers who can sell a 'comb to the bald' promising comfort in management and the load comes on the Executors and Doers.

What is the component of 'real' work and 'fancy' work that an average Doer is doing in my organisation?

This is a real management task, today. The facilities available today should have reduced the load on humans, but the facts are contrary to the expectations. Organisations need to shed their 'time wasters' and drastically and ruthlessly cut the working time.

Productivity will shoot up.

Let us rethink and rework to reduce "tension" to increase "productivity".

CREATIVITY OR CONSISTENCY?

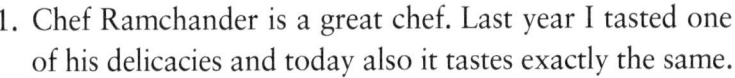

1. Chef Ramchander is a great chef. Last year I tasted one of his delicacies and today also it tastes exactly the same.
2. Radha is great at typing. She types @70 wpm without any mistake.
3. My driver is excellent. He always keeps the speed in the fixed range and is always in control.
4. The shooter Gyanji is a great shooter. He has been practising for the same gun event for past 9 years.
5. The bank cashier Shahji can count lakhs of notes in minutes.
6. The painter Ashok in the trade fair can make your sketch in minutes.
7. The salesperson has to make 25 calls with same script every day.
8. The production guy is supposed to follow the same norms day in and day out.
9. The orchestra team has to follow the notes as it is in the same rhythm, everyone.
10. The singer has to exactly follow the pattern given by the music director.

11. The actor Siddhartha perfectly plays the role of Robert on stage. He has been the star performer for the last 7 years.

Most of the actions which get appreciation and results are based on the creativity of a few followed by a very, very long period of consistency by many. Repetitions bring excellence. A small creativity, to be useful, needs to be followed by a long, long slog of unsung consistency.

> *'When we talk of life, business, and management consistency should always come before creativity.'*
> *- AB-MFH*

At times one act of creativity needs years of consistent effort by a big team to make it a business worthy idea. A small team of 4 engineers developed a creative design of an automobile. A plant of hundreds of workers, a sales network, and service centres all over worked consistently for years to make it a business success.

In business, at times, overdose of creativity can be very expensive. Converting creativity into a business opportunity and then making it happen is the real challenge. At times it is very expensive too. Further, *most of the times it is possible to outsource creativity, but it is not so with consistency.* Management education needs to focus more on this. The real challenge for any business and any management is to maintain this.

> *Business management is primarily a dish of consistency flavoured with seasoning of creativity.*

ASK, ASK, AND ASK

I always like to differentiate leaders into good leaders and not-so-good leaders.

*What exactly is the difference between a **good leader** and a **not-so-good leader**?*

Well not much!

To me the main difference between the two is that the good leader never gets tired of ASKING while a not-so-good leader gets exhausted by the act of ASKING.

Today also my mother, even after I am fifty plus, keeps on asking -

whether I have taken my meals,

am I taking sufficient rest,

do I come home on time?

and so on...

Remember, when a kid is running away from the mother who is trying to feed him.

Does she tire of trying to feed him?

Does she complain that he is not taking food properly even after years of this follow-up?

Does she ever give-up?
This is great leadership.
It is not important as to how many times I have to follow this. It is important that I must follow till the desired minimum result is achieved.

I must 'ask.... ask.... and ask' and still if the job is not done then ask again.

A not-so-good leader may get tired after asking once, twice, five times, ten times, but a good leader never gets tired of asking. That is one most important management tools and often is the least propagated one. Some people raise brows when I insist that the main task of a leader is 'to ask'. They often resist, the followers are supposed to obey or abide by it. It should not be required to ask so much. My contention is that it is not a question of so much or so little. It is the matter of results. If you get result by asking one time, it's fine. Thanks. But, if you have to ask a number of times, don't panic, you have to, that's your job.

Following up is part of leaders' job. Now you are the leader...

HANDLING UNCERTAINITY

'UNCERTAINTY'

There are very uncertain definitions about this word. Some define it as a state of being doubtful and some call it a state of being uncertain. The definitions itself are very uncertain.

But it is a very important aspect of life, business, and management.

I like to define it as –

> 'A situation where in I have no choice, or I have many choices which either I am incapable of comparing or I am unable to compare'.

So, what do I do?

Either I must fight with this word uncertainty, get over it, remove it, and move further into certainty, else I have to handle uncertainty.

To handle uncertainty, I go with the above definition.

Why I am uncertain if I have no choice? When I have no choice and I know that then it is not an uncertainty.

In the second case, if I am unable or incapable of comparing and that is creating the uncertainty then any choice is equally good or equally bad.

If I am venturing into an unknown territory, then I am certain that it is an unknown territory. There is no question of expecting certainty here.

There is a third case, where I am trying to make a fool of myself in front of myself. I want to do 'A' and data, or logic is calling for 'B'.

I flip a coin.

call B B B B B B B B B.

and do B.

Certainly.

Simple but not easy.

THE GOLD MEDAL

'The largest selling commodity on this planet Earth is comfort.'
Anything which is associated with comfort is easily accepted and people are willing to pay exorbitantly higher prices for the same. Comfort is such a commodity for which man can sacrifice his health, his consciousness, and even his sanity.

Then why do people
scale Mount Everest,
take part in Olympics, or
join the armed forces.

There is something more than comfort that urges people towards these goals, something more to the story. The feeling of being important is stronger than being in the comfort zone. All types of activities from being a sports hero, to being screen hero, to being political leaders, to being terrorist all stem from the psychological need to feel important.

In business and industry, we have to propel people towards uncomfortable levels. We will have to bring people out of the comfort zones to achieve excellence. The motivational factor for this journey is the feeling of being important. Many a times we associate this urge for importance with money as well.

> *No doubt money is important but more than money it is the status associated with money.*
>
> *Another very big motivation is the Gold Medal.*

HISTORY OF THE GOLD MEDAL

The system of gold, silver, and bronze medals has been existing for ages now and it has been a successful motivator, generation after generation. This is the only grading system that has stood for centuries and has kept on motivating masses year after year, generation after generation. Everyone aspires for the gold. After any event there are four categories

Gold winners,
Silver winners,
Bronze winners and
Also, those who simply ran or the participants.

People in all the four categories work hard and train to their best. They work consistently for years for the Gold, which will be secured only by one of them. Some people who got silver or bronze medals may have trained and worked even better than the one who got the gold.

The difference between the four is not very big. But the value difference between the awards is

0
400
40000
4000000.

And this DIFFERENCE & ASSOCIATED STATUS is what has kept generations aspiring and being motivated for the GOLD.

Can we use this as a management tool?

MANAGEMENTS RESPONSIBILITY - THE NO MAN THE NO MAN

'I' and 'No', are the two smallest words in the vocabulary. Both are very dangerous, but the latter is more critical. *It relieves the user from answerability and responsibility and shifts the onus on the person saying 'YES'.* The person using 'NO' will never falter as he needs to do nothing. He will always have time to find excuses and logics.

I had a HR head as a NO MAN.

'I have to go to Delhi. Should I go by air?'

HR: 'No'.

'You suggest.'

HR: 'It's your job'.

'Ok, I'll take a cab'.

HR: 'No'.

'You suggest.'

HR: 'It's your job'.

'Ok, I'll take the bus'.

HR: 'No'.

'You suggest.'

HR: 'It's your job.'

'Ok, I'll go on foot'!

HR: 'I will put a note that you are wasting your valuable time by going on foot'.

As part of the management, it is my prime responsibility to safeguard the 'DOERS' from the 'NO MAN'. It is also my responsibility to see that the NO-MAN is sufficiently performing. The poor performance of a no-man is not only his poor performance, but it also creates a situation where he will try to mar and overshadow the doers. They can't do it and will not allow others who can, to do it. To identify and take care, to not allow such people to disturb the harmony of the system, is one of the primary tasks of the management.

> Be-aware: "There is always a right logic to justify every wrong".

DYNAMICS OF A CONSENSUS MEETING

I am sitting in a very important MEETING. There are twenty participants and a hot discussion is on. Disconnected for some time, I was lost in my thoughts when I found myself having the 'spectator's view'. From this view I found that a meeting has various types of participants.

One category, like me were not involved at all. Probably they don't know why they were in. These participants were constantly moving in and out of the process, mentally. Yawning with tightly pressed lips, constantly moving in their chairs – *the indifferents.*

There is one category of people who are soft spoken and who really know the subject matter. They have the right answers, but they have low voice levels and are weak public speakers – *the reals.*

Wait. Here are some participants who are also very soft spoken, cool participants having a very descent intellectual smiles much like the reals. A close observation reveals that they are only silent spectators, pretending to be reals – *the imposters.*

There is one variety of homo sapiens who can steer the whole team to a faraway distant destination – *the wanderers.*

The fourth category – they are loud people who know something about the subject but more than the knowledge, they are very good at presentations – *the presenter.*

Now this is the most dangerous one.
They have a specific point of view. They are rigid on it. They don't have ears and are also senior by post – *the arrogants.*

The sixth are, what we call 'BRINJAL ON A PLATE'. They constantly move with the inclination, mostly with the mood swings of the meeting head. They do not have any stand or logic of their own – *the rollers.*

There are some participants who are completely unrelated – *the guests.*

Some are in for entertainment like for trekking to a tourist spot, for amusement only – *the tourists.*

And how can I forget the members who always move with the wind. They are ultimately going to play a vital role in the final outcome – *the politicians.*

Do I need to explain what is going to be the course of this meeting?

The point here is that the selection of participants and the control of the meeting head are vital for the success of any meeting. The participants of a consensus building meeting have to be strictly directly concerned members only. *Simple but never easy.*

THE PANACEA OF DECISION-MAKING

A panacea – is one solution that will solve all problems. I have this typical problem. I want one solution to all my problems. As the head of an organisation, I am supposed to solve the, so called, problems of all the team members. Ideally, I know, that I should support decision-making at much lower levels but how is it possible that something happens in MY organisation without my knowledge. So, the situation now is that everything comes to me for decision-making.

This leads to another issue – *I want that I should take all the decisions but the team members (I like to call them leaders!) should be responsible for it. A very typical problem.*

I lived with this for years till I found A PANACEA. What? CONSENSUS!

A solution to all decision-making issues.

Why we humans always want to make things easy?

Now I have a way to impose my decision and push the responsibility on Mr X. Irrespective of the type of problem or issue. Now how to build consensus. Let us call all concerned, 'less concerned', and 'not-so-concerned' to discuss.

'HOW SHOULD I GO TO DELHI FOR A MEETING?'

I have to take a call. I have 4 options: car, flight, train and bus. A very difficult call indeed. Ok. I have a great tool. I will do a SWOT analysis.

Yep!

OPTION 1 – CAR

STRENGTHS	OPPORTUNITIES
Independence.	Can do some other jobs on the way.
Convenience of local traveling.	To test the driving skills of the driver.
Time flexibility.	Check the mileage of my car.
From home to back.	
Breakfast at my favourite spot.	…………
…………	**THREATS**
WEAKNESSES	Accident.
Need driver.	Puncture or any maintenance issue.
Expensive.	Dacoits (? which era but maybe???)
I have to remain alert to watch the driver.	…………
Not comfortable to do writing work.	
…………	

Similar SWOTs of flight, bus, and train can be prepared.

NOW WHAT?

Now I am more intelligent.

I know that every option has some strengths, some weaknesses, some opportunities, and some threats.

BUT WHAT ABOUT THE DECISION?

It is more confusing. How can I compare? Every option has some weaknesses and some threats?

I have to find a way to improve decision-making.

Help!

'HOW SHOULD I GO TO DELHI FOR A MEETING?'

We call 6 panellists to take the decision, through consensus.

AWARENESS ROUND

My secretary prepares detailed note on

The purpose

The 'what,

The 'why and how', and

The agenda…

Character sketch of the person whom I have to meet.

Objection – it is not 'what', 'why and how', it is 'why', 'what and how'!

STUDY ROUND

All panellists are given time to study; 6 days is just sufficient. One real serious type actually goes to Delhi and to the venue too. One goes to check the seating in the buses, car, train, and plane. A sincere hardworking team.

BRAINSTORMING

Simply brilliant. We have a 5X6' white board. Let everybody give suggestions. And the session starts. A long 60 mins session. Board was full of options we need extra sheets! There were great, out-of-the-box ideas like walking, taking lift, a combo package also. Someone also suggested cancelling or inviting the gentleman here.

Now from 4 options I have 24.

Unthinkable!

Really, I could not have done so much thinking.

The journey continues. Most of the 6 team members are now dire enemies not on talking terms. 6 months later the meetings are on. I am waiting...

'HOW SHOULD I GO TO DELHI FOR A MEETING?'

And this really happens!!!

THE CRITICAL CCTV

I was sitting in my friend's office who is the owner of a manufacturing unit. On the wall opposite to him, behind my head, were 10 screens. He was able to see almost every corner of his office space through 4X10' screens. During my first 30 mins in his office, I could sense a strange restlessness in his behaviour. He was not like that earlier. Since we are school friends, I could ask him to shut all the screens and asked him to discuss the issue.

He told me that since his business has started growing so he felt a need to hire a senior helping hand. Almost eight months back he hired a senior person who told him that his team members were simply loitering and wasting time. They won't listen to him and so he quit. Before leaving he arranged this CCTV arrangement for me.

But you have a wonderful team?

Yes, that was exactly what I used to think before I had this.

He was in deep trouble now – 'the doubt cycle' had started playing.

How much was your turnover to manpower ratio last year? Obviously, he did not have the figures. I told him to get these figures on monthly basis for last 3 years. Then I asked him to switch the CCTV off for 6 months. 'Next week I will come again you keep the data ready.'

As expected, the CCTV period was the worst one. I asked him to share the data with the team and declare that you have decided to say goodbye to the CCTV.

We met yesterday after more than 6 months and he is happy. His team is happy, and they are growing together.

Nutshell: "Have your control points and check points and go by them, let the CCTV be for what it is meant for".

Remember: Work energizes, tension drains.

THE CONFIDANT

'A CONFIDANT is a trusted friend who you can talk to about personal and private things.'

When I was a bachelor, I used to shop for myself, sometimes alone sometimes with some friends. I liked light pink colour shirts. All through my single days I always kept a few pink shirts and I treasured them. Then I got married and same continued for a few years. After about three years of marriage, once while shopping and obviously the pink shirt, my wife slowly told me that pink didn't suit me. I looked dark in pink and white was a better alternative.

I was shocked. After reaching home I took out all my shirts, one by one tried them and asked my wife (now my CONFIDANTE) to take my pictures. Then we sat together and analysed them. *I was surprised to find that all those shirts which I had purchased myself did not suit me, to lesser or more extent, and the ones which were bought for me by others or after consultation were the ones that suited me the most.*

If my CONFIDANT is true in the matter of shirt selection, which I can see in the mirror or in the picture, then what about the matters which I do without being able to see the consequences?

That is the value of a CONFIDANT. Like I expressed in case of Spectators' view, *the Confidant's view is very important and having a CONFIDANT is the most important treasure.*

THE MFH - METHOD OF DECISION- MAKING

'SINGULAR INCLUSIVE' - *The MFH method for decision-making*

Are there various methods of decision-making?

Sure, depending upon the participation level there are different methods of decision-making, like:

1. Through consensus,
2. Through discussion,
3. Through autocracy,
4. Through democracy,
5. Through expert (internal),
6. Through expert (external) and
   maybe a few more.

All these can be broadly summed up in two categories

1. Singular
2. Plural

Theoretically speaking, ideal is the plural method. More is covered in the portion on 'meeting dynamics', but in a nutshell it boils down to the 'everybody, nobody, anybody, somebody' story.

Here we will discuss the practically best method of decision-making, obviously it is singular and MFH has suggested the name Singular inclusive method. When it is singular through expert then there is no need for discussion.

The question is singular, how?

MFH calls this as 'SINGULAR INCLUSIVE' method of decision-making. Simply put, the steps defined (only guidelines and not rules) are:

1. Find a 'suitable' person for the job.
2. **Nominate and declare the person responsible and accountable for the decision.**
3. The person is supposed to study and collect as much knowledge as possible.
4. He/she can talk, discuss, and take views of all members concerned individually.
5. He/she should (may) take joint meetings of 'only directly concerned' team members.
6. He/she has to be associated from beginning to the end of the process.
7. He/she has to take the decision.
8. He/she is responsible for communicating the decision to all 'concerned'.

No questions please...

THE HIERARCHY

CONVENTIONAL HIERARCHY	MFH - HIERARCHY ORGANISATION "X"
Top management (The leader?)	Doers
Senior management	Supervisor (The leader)
Middle management	Provider level 1
Operations management	Provider level 2
Supervisor	Guide
Doers	Expander (Top management)

Every level of hierarchy has its own role in the organisation. For clarity of thought let us start from the Doers. *The Doers are the real working hands, feet, and minds. There is a fourth feature which is normally ignored at all hierarchy levels – the heart. The vision of the top management is executed by the doers.*

The Operation/supervisory management is normally upgraded from doers or qualified people either fresh or with a couple of years' experiences in managing. But they have specific skill training. Those who are at this level are translating all the requirements of the organisation in a language understandable by the doers. *They are directly witnessing and guiding the Doers.* **They are the REAL LEADERS.**

The Middle management is the first and second **provider level.** It is their responsibility to guide the operation/supervisory levels. They have to arrange for the necessary inputs for them including knowledge, technology, equipment, tools, manpower, etc. They are also the planners of the ongoing activities. They have to ensure that the teams are able to perform to the expectations of **the 'X'.**

The senior management is the think tank. They are the guides, the coaches, the mentors. They also translate the vision of **the 'X'** into comprehensive language. They guide the juniors to perform and they guide the top management to envision. They also verbalise and plan the vision of **the 'X'.**

The Top management has to be always in the expansion mode. They are the Kings and the Emperors, and **the 'X'** looks upon them for growth, upgradation, and expansion, always, every time.

Who is the 'X'?

Yes this 'X' is above all, the Zenith of the hierarchy. It is *'THE ORGANISATION'.*

THE CHRONIC
MICRO-MANAGER

I am/was a micro-manager. All my well-wishers always tried directly or indirectly to tell me and bring me out of this habit. One well-wisher even gave me a management book which illustrated the issue of micro-management very well on my birthday. I am explaining this to reveal that I am aware that I am a micro-manager. One day I decided that I will do away with this tendency. I decided to start with my assistant. I have a document box. My assistant operates it to keep in and take out some (but not very) important documents. I keep the keys. I go with him when the box is to be opened and stand there, obviously commenting, till the box is closed and keys handed over.

This will be my starting point to exit the micro-management practices. With many questions related to the 'ifs', I called my subordinate, 'I am giving you this box. From today you are the custodian. You are authorised to keep anything and take out any content. Here is the lock and the key. Everything is under your authority from today onwards.'

Subordinate thanked me, was about to leave with the locked box and the keys when I handed him instructions manual for using the box which read -

'Every time you open the box to keep in or take out anything from this box you have to call one security person, stores manager, accounts officer, and (me).'

Disclaimer: This is not a work of fiction; it is based on many true stories. Stories which are going to continue even after...

TWO HANDS
MULTIPLY

An owner once said, 'I have 1000 hands working for me.'

The second one said, 'I have 1000 hands and 1000 feet working for me.'

The third boasted, 'I have 1000 hands, 1000 feet, and 500 brains working for me.'

Further

The fourth came in and said, 'I have 1000 hands, 1000 feet, 500 brains, and 500 hearts working for me'.

But a typical traditional Indian businessman's view was -

'I am fortunate to help 500 families to live happily. We are working together to create a wonderful future for all'.

This idea is going to be the backbone of the future of the world, led by the Gen Z. This tradition had made India 'sone ki chidiya' (the bird of gold).

HIRING –
THE RIGHT WAY

HIRING – SHEEP, HORSES, OR ELEPHANTS

Hiring is the most important activity for any organisation and very few give it its due importance. It is like giving birth to a child. The organisation is supposed to be the mother for the lifetime for the employee.

> *MFH divides different activities in any organisation as –*
>
> *Sheep, Horse, and Elephant work.*
>
> *Accordingly, the Supervisors, the Managers, the department Heads are the –*
>
> *Shepherd, Jockey, and Mahout.*

Whenever I have to hire a person, I first identify his position based on the above six categories. Before doing this type of classification I was normally hiring horses (as they are good at interviews) for sheep work, or sheep for elephant work

I also committed errors like hiring a jockey in place of horse, again because he was obviously very good at the interview designed for horses.

You should not put a sheep in the herd of elephants and expect great results. Worst conditions are placing an elephant in the shoes of a shepherd. This is the basic reason for politics, unrest, and chaos. Then we complain about inefficiency. For apparently similar positions such as engineer for process control, engineer for quality control, and engineer for maintenance or marketing the categorization could be different.

The first few months after recruiting are also very important. We have to induct and train each category differently. This will be dealt with later.

MANAGEMENT VS SPORTS: DECISION-TAKING

I was reading an article on 'decision-making' written for management personals. The author very articulately explained how a tennis star improved his game and won many grand slam titles by taking special training for sharp, quick, and accurate decision-taking. It was a wonderful read.

The only issue is that I am unable to correlate the relationship between decision-taking in the tennis game with management decision-taking.

Normally, decision-taking in sports is a split-second event. The decisions can be programmed into muscle memory – the reflex action. It is the speed that is important. The decision taker and the executor is the same, the process is largely individualistic. The coach can be of help only during training and practising. During the event he is also a spectator. The decision and its result are almost instantaneous. The decision taker practises off the field for hours, every day for months and years.

> *Management on the other hand is not an event. It is a process. There is no split second, reflex, decision to be taken here.*

We have time to study, discuss, take views, and reviews. The process is in no way correlated with the other one. The impact of a management decision may take years to fructify. The decision may, most of the times, impact a very large number of people. The impact can be within and outside of the organisation and there are no practice sessions.

PROBLEM-SOLVING TOOLS

There are no problems!

Wow!

What a start to the topic on problem solving tools?

So, I need to go to Delhi from Amloh, two places 300 kms apart. I can go by car, bus, train, or flight. Then what's the problem? I can't decide. I am confused and I am unable to decide.

Fine. So, we have a problem. Let us see if our problem-solving tools will help here.

Let's apply problem solving.

Ok, we start with one of the most useful tools - brainstorming. I call my 20 teammates to the meeting hall. I am on the whiteboard. They start bombarding suggestions and soon the whiteboard is unable to handle the data.

End of the session.

I have 24 more ideas from going on foot, to call the other person here, to cancel the trip!

Great session. I would never have assumed that there were so many alternatives.

Did my tool help?

'Problem solving tools help to get probable solutions if you don't know the alternatives.'

> *Is this a PROBLEM or is it a case of an issue with a PENDING DECISION or MY INDECISIVENESS?*
>
> *In most (maybe 99.9% or more) of the cases we try to call 'pending decision' a problem. No problem-solving tool can help in such a situation.*

MOTIVATION- A HUMAN CHARACTERISTIC

> *Being motivated is an intrinsic human characteristic.*
> *For us humans, motivation is parallel to breathing.*
> For breathing it is essential to have fresh air around and
> we feel choked in a polluted atmosphere. The same is
> true for motivation. The negativity in the atmosphere
> around us chokes our motivation.

Building an atmosphere which promotes higher levels of
motivation in the team members is a prime responsibility
of the top management, in other words this is called
building a great organisation culture. A good organisation
culture supports the motivation level of all team members.
The four main motivation maintainers are-

1. A home with capability to provide sufficient resources
   to the family members with respect to status level of
   the family in the society.
2. Trust of the management followed by regular
   reassurances.

3. Sufficient opportunity to improve and demonstrate ever higher capabilities. An opportunity to grow.

4. *Constantly upgrading the not-so-comfortable 'comfort zone'. Nobody wants to be stuck in his so-called comfort zone. Everyone wants the management to help them to rise to the next 'uncomfortable zone'.*

I always thought that people don't want to leave their comfort zones, but I was wrong. In fact, the opportunity to leave the comfort zone without disturbing the family's compulsions and needs is a big motivation booster.

We should consider this critical factor while formulating guidelines (MFH prefers to call policies as guidelines).

MY IDENTITY

Many a times I hear people saying that *'keep your work separate and your life separate.'*

Is it possible?

My life is 24 hours every day - 24X7, 365.25 days a year.

Where and why should I take 8, 10, 12 or more hours of my life out of my life?

Is it possible?

When we meet someone for the first time how do we introduce ourselves:

MY INTRO

1. *I am Anil Bhatia (name)*

2. *I stay in / I belong to Amloh (place)*

3. *I work with Madhav Alloys Ltd as VP (Operations)*

   "NAME, PLACE, AND WORK"

That's it.
I don't say:
I am the son of...
I am the husband of...
I am the brother of...
I am the father of...
Even an unemployed person will say -
I am Anil Bhatia (name).
I stay in / I belong to Amloh (place).
I am unemployed (work).
Our work is our identity.

Let us all do justice to our work. Let us consider our work, our jobs as part of our lives.

MFH says that we must enjoy our work as we enjoy other parts of our life. Enjoy Mondays as you enjoy Sundays. Consider your office to be your home. Treat your seniors like parents, uncles, grandpa, grandma. Your peers you're your brother, sister, cousins, and friends. Your subordinates like your kids, your brother's kids.

If we don't forget that 'my work is my identity', life will be different.

It will be a new experience, altogether.

DANGEROUS DELAY

THE STORY

My son, 'I secured the first place in the exams!'

My reaction, 'Go to the yard and chop woods. This your punishment.'

My son, 'But I...'

Me, 'This is for the fight you had with our neighbour's son 4 months and 36 days back.'

And at some other time...

My neighbour, 'Your son rammed your car into my fence.'

Me, 'Here son take keys of your new bike.'

Neighbour, 'For breaking my fence?'

Me, 'No, no. It's for the race he won last December.'

Both the above incidents appear grossly idiotic. Are you sure?

I do the same regularly in my organisation. We rarely feel anything wrong in doing so in our day to day management of organisations. How often we wait for 'The meeting', 'The PMS', 'The review session' to give such feedbacks, pat-on-the-back, reprimands, etc.

I don't know how much damage these 'post-mortem meetings' are giving to many wonderful, potentially great organisations?

Meetings are a great 'tool' for future planning and decision propagating, sometimes decision-making also. They give a bigger interaction platform. But they are not a substitute for one-to-one conversations and interactions. One line/ word remark - 'Great job!' or 'No!' at the right time cannot be replaced by hours of post incident meetings.

Why does this happen?

Why are we not able to see this simple logic in the organisations while we are doing the same in our homes?

The possible reason is the inability to pass on the ownership. When I am rewarding my son, it is my decision, my call and so I can take it. But does my organisation give me the same ownership when it comes to my team members. This can be the game changer.

Normally it is considered that the team of contractual workers perform better than the direct employees.

Yes, it is so.

But why?

The difference lies in the above-mentioned simple philosophy. The contractors delegate and empower much more than the full-time employees of the organized organisations. They virtually make their site heads as their proxies, the decision-making is at right time, and the results are obvious.

We need to learn from the Contractors some basic management lessons.

DO I KNOW WHAT I DON'T KNOW?

I am an entrepreneur. My business involves purchase, finance, stores, production... I am a simple graduate engineer, a simple human being with normally normal everything - 2 eyes, 2 ears, and 24 hours per day like anybody else.

How can I know everything required to run a business?

How do I know what I don't know?

Well, I have to work hard!

How can I tell my purchase manager that I don't know from where and at what price 'XYZ BUTTON 35mmX62mm' can be purchased best?

If I don't know the best how can I guide him? Just a look at our father and mother, they do purchase, accounts, finance, budgeting, stores, inventory management. What I need as a leader is a good team and my check points. I can hire extensions to my faculties. I can take views and advice. At some point I can be an assistant to my purchase manager and at other point I can help my sales manager.

What to do with what I don't know? First, I need to know what I don't know and then I need to know who knows it. The first part is more difficult. As a leader, entrepreneur or manager, understanding your own limitations and seeking support is most important. Only then you can positively search for sources of information and guidance.

WE FORGIVE AND FORGET OUR CHILDREN

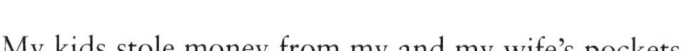

My kids stole money from my and my wife's pockets.

Did they become professional thieves?

No.

Today they are responsible adults.

Did we throw them out of the house or hand them over to the police?

Not at all.

They are responsible citizens today.

Do we still hold a grudge against them?

Never.

We forgive our children.

At best, we make them aware that we know what they have done.

We educate them to be good, responsible citizens.

We give them our time.

We develop a rapport with them.

We deal with them patiently.

We observe their behaviour and actions.

Gradually we start demonstrating our trust.

Slowly we allow the trust to develop.

We forgive and forget the incident.

Simple but not easy.

It needs your time and dedication.

Every parent educated, uneducated, engineer, manager, or entrepreneur does the same. This needs no formal degree or course to learn. This is natural.

The same is equally true in management. We are also related to our subordinates, colleagues, and seniors. The basics remain the same, but we try to handle them differently.

ONE PASSIONATE PERSON

'One passionate person can help hundreds of people with positive attitude to accomplish just anything'

Nothing can replace passion.

Attitude cannot.

Aptitude cannot.

Knowledge cannot.

Skill cannot.

Passion will drive you to build your Attitude.

It will force you to acquire

Aptitude

Knowledge

Skill

Plus, whatever is required.

Passion deletes all boundaries and limitations and gives us the strength to resist all resistances.

Just be passionate about your passion.

SHOW POSITIVE MANAGEMENT RESPONSIBILITY

This is a very important management responsibility which has tremendous power to transform the ordinary into the extraordinary.

THE STORY

There were two sales managers in a company with both of them having 5 salesmen each. The teams were given the same training, same tools, and similar territories. A year later it was found that the team of Rakeshji was consistently performing better than Ashokji's team.

A close analysis of their interactions with their teams revealed that -

Rakeshji

always focussed on the team members' success stories.

He always asked them, in detail, why and how they were successful in getting this deal closed.

He did not allow a discussion on failures.

In fact, he used to shut members who even tried to discuss or justify failures.

How a team member was able to successfully handle a tough client, was discussed within the team.

What went right was always the focus.

Ashokji, on the contrary

was always discussing reasons for failure.

What they can learn from the experience of an unsuccessful deal. They conducted review sessions to discuss 'what could have been done to avoid the failure'.

What went wrong was the focus of the team.

The team was actually trying to re-live an unsuccessful venture to delve the reasons for the failure.

What went wrong was always the focus.

The intention of both the leaders was good. Both want to boost their company's sales, and both were very dedicated members and are working hard to produce the desired results.

'We cannot expect to bring any positive change by continuously showing, discussing, and highlighting the negative points. Knowing the right way is more important than knowing the wrong one in life, business, and management.'

RULES V/S GUIDELINES

Rules,	Guidelines,
Give a sense of being controlled.	on the other hand
Being incapable, immature,	Give responsibility.
and dominion.	Bring self-respect to the fore.
A lack of authority.	Encourage improvement.
An identity loss.	Support belongingness.
When broken, even inadvertently, gives a guilty feeling.	Give direction.
Makes us resentful.	Make us sombre.

Rules are important at some places but in the world of business and management, MFH finds that *'guidelines' outshine 'rules'*.

Let us try it.

Gradually start replacing a few 'rules' with 'guidelines' and declare that openly to all the team members. I am sure that the results will be astonishing, and your organisation will move to the next level effortlessly.

Catch: all rules are not replaceable but most of them are.

A CAR WITH A MIRROR IN PLACE OF WINDSCREEN

'Life, business, and management are like driving a car with mirror in place of windscreen'

Venturing into a new project, spending two years studying the intricacies, after preparing an exhaustive 700+ page report, discussing with several experts, I thought that I was ready to launch.

Tomorrow I have to give the presentation. All the board members are mostly convinced so it will be a simple formality to declare the final launch date.

Casually I was talking to my daughter, who has just completed her Masters in Mass Communication, in the evening. Her interest and my curiosity converted into a long lecture on how our team had worked on the project. Our visits to China, Austria, Italy, and our market surveys, etc.

'But all this is historical data?'

Her question!!!

'Yes.'

That's how it is done.

We always try to drive into the future looking at a map that is only showing the path which has already been travelled. All our studies are attempts to decipher the future using the information of the past. The worst part is that most of the times we are overconfident that we are capable of forecasting.

We have to always be aware of the fact that we are driving with a mirror in place of a windscreen.

Just for a few minutes close your eyes and visualise that you are the driver with your seat and steering wheel turned backwards.

Imagine that you are driving the reverse gear.

How far you see the road?

A few meters only?

Can we really rely on projections of the road ahead with the map of the road traversed?

Definitely we cannot, but surely, we can be aware of this situation. Are we aware?

DIFFICULTY V/S NECESSARY

When confronted with a difficult decision simply ask yourself 'is it necessary', if the answer is 'yes' difficulty will vanish.

Management of all types require firmness. Some type of discipline (it may be different from the conventional design - covered elsewhere in MFH). We have to be a blend of good, firm, and not-so-good. We cannot always move with 'good-man' tags.

- At times we have to take tough calls too.
- Many times, we have to choose one out of many probables.
- We also may have to remove an old team member.
- Take some disciplinary actions or reprimand.

Many more such calls.

Often, we find that we are stuck with such so called unpleasant decisions. I also used to find them difficult to take. At times, before delivering the decision to fire some old member, I used to have sleepless nights. Now I know that it is common with most senior decision takers. Often you see senior people calling at morning odd hours and giving not-so-pleasant sermons. Now I understand their state of mind.

Is it a correct behaviour?

Can we do something to handle this situation in a better way?

Yes. Surely.

I got this solution in "Gandhari Geeta".

When confronted with a difficult decision simply ask yourself 'is it necessary', if the answer is "yes" difficulty will vanish. You can try...

TODAY DECIDES TOMORROW

My targets, my vision, my goals are not going to make me reach them. I don't believe that Jamshedji Tata, Dhirubhai Ambani, or for that matter the founders of any of today's giant businesses 'targeted' where they are today.

In todays' system, we are over-emphasising the concepts of targets, goals, and aims. Let us try to imagine the owner of a giant organisation when he started in a small or mediocre way. In a small space with a few team members, out to make a living for self and family. A dream; we all have dreams.

What different they did when compared to innumerable others who 'also ran'?

They planned their present.
They maximised the present.
They surpassed the conceivable and visualisable.
They had a wonderful sense of detachment to allow them to move forward.

They invariably had a three step, simple program.

1. The first step is to look for a business opportunity and go all out in establishing it.
2. The second one is to find or develop an enthusiastic team with a positive attitude to take care of the establishment and to empower them. They knew that their job is establishing and venturing. They are best at that. They did not try to run the show.
3. The third obvious step was to find a new business opportunity. Do step 1 and 2 again and again and again.

Very simple 3 steps to build a business empire. *The second step is like a partial moksha, detachment. Without this, re-visiting step 1 is not possible.*

Any organisation should have three distinct teams, accordingly.

One being new opportunity seeker (Change management),

Second, the establisher (Consistency management) and

The third operator (All-is-well management).

The owner has to be the part of the first one. The attitude of the three teams is also distinct.

'They did not focus on the future; they did their best today and definitely maximised the present.'

THE WARNING SIGNALS

- The person who is obviously responsible for taking a particular decision does not take it.
- Team members either refrain from or do not respond to 'light notes and jokes' on the group WhatsApp.
- The team members who are lower in hierarchy do not invite the top management to their major family functions like their weddings or the weddings of their children, etc.
- *Any NEWS posted by seniors get many thumbs up reactions instantaneously but a similar NEWS posted by juniors gets a thumbs-up only after acknowledgement by the top bosses.*
- A senior member starts asking for reports and justifications for obvious occurrences.
- Coming early and overstaying becomes a norm.
- *Team members stop taking half days for their children's parent-teacher meetings.*
- Junior team members shirk to meet the top management members at public places.

- Simple, low cost facilities like tea, snacks, pen, stationery etc. start becoming scarce and topics of discussion.
- Communication gets replaced by unidirectional instructions and orders.
- *There is a reduction in informal meetings, but there are ever increasing formal structured meetings.*
- Inter-personal topics getting discussed in joint meetings.
- TA bills getting over-scrutinised and discussed.
- Casual attitude (चलता है) creeps in and is especially marked in erstwhile sincere team members.
- When my personal purchases are different from organisational procurements. I buy brand 'X' for Rs. 1000/- for my home and for the organisation I buy brand 'Y', an inferior brand for Rs. 999/-. Cost shadows value.
- When local transporters and vendors stop giving priority to our organisation needs.
- *When procedures become excuses for inefficiency.*
- When secrecy creeps in place of openness.
- Discussions turn into debates.
- The erstwhile serious and participative members fall into the silent mode.

FROM EVENT TO PROCESS

Life, business, and management is a journey of continuously moving from 'event' to 'process.'

An Event is something that happens or is made to happen in a time zone. It is an occurrence which has a beginning and an end.

It may end without any associated impact,
it may end (which happens many times) in a win/lose,
it may end with a compromise,
it may end in a win-win.

A Process is a series of events which are identified to give a predetermined result when performed in a fixed order. A process is identified by its repeatability and consequently permanence.

Life, business, and management is a continuous cycle of converting events to processes.

When we start a new concept, the stage from idea to implementation is an event. The event concludes with the successful output of the concept. Thereafter it needs to be transformed into a process to get the desired output again and again, continuously, perennially. Here it is important to mention that 'change' is part of the event stage and 'improvement' is normally part of the process.

The philosophy of management of an event is at gross variance with the philosophy of management of a process.

> *"CHANGE" is part of the event stage and "IMPROVEMENT" is normally part of the process.*
> *AB-MFH*

Management of an event may involve

Creativity
Versatility
Frequent change
Maximisation
Variability
Quick decision-making
Unidirectional
But

Management of a process involves

Consistency
Repeatability
No change, only modification
Optimisation
Long term planning
Continuity
Cyclical
Definitely
Management is simple but not easy.

WHY IS TRUSTING SO DIFFICULT?

I have been asking this question in most of my classes, 'Is there anyone in the room who wants that he or she should not be trusted?'

For last 35 years I am trying to find one person who wants that he should 'not' be trusted. All in vain. I want to be trusted but I cannot trust. When everybody wants and wants with all sincerity that one should be trusted than why do we find it so difficult to trust?

Strange.

Yes, this is very strange indeed. We all want that we should be trusted but we find it difficult to trust others.

Why? Why is it so?

Possibly a perception error.

We always misidentify 'trust' with its counter - 'blind faith'.

It is good to trust, but it never implies blind faith. Trust is a bond builder, a positive approach requiring positive leadership, whereas blind faith is a result of 'lethargic leadership'.

- We trust our children when we first leave their hands when they are taking their first steps.
- We trust them when we leave them in school to attend their first class.
- We trust them when we leave the carrier of their first cycle.
- We trust them with pocket money.
- We trust them when they go to hostels.

But we never have blind faith on them. We watch them and we tell them that they need not worry we are watching. This further strengthens the trust. Parents always trust their children; they never exhibit blind faith in them. They never confuse trust with blind faith.

> *But when it is the question of our organisations and that of our subordinates, we perceive trust as a process where we are supposed to close our eyes and ears and have blind faith.*

COMMUNICATION - TRANSFERRING INTENTION

'Transferring intention' is a very important ingredient in the process of developing and maintaining the organisation culture, an important management task.

Like with all communication, we often treat emailing, writing, or at best calling over the phone as communication done. Same holds for the 'most' crucial *'communicating intention'*.

We all are familiar with the game 'Chinese whisper' or 'Telephone'. The message given by the initiator gets distorted en route. This is not a game but a practical reality - the biggest management issue. In the game, the messages given are normally very simple single or two liners and still, they get grossly distorted during the *transfer process*.

> *Did you ever realise what happens with your complex instructions, orders, information, and intention transfer that you are passing to your team members through various messaging tools?*

How can we reduce the distortion in information transfer?

Complex? No.

Difficult? Yes.

I never said 'management is easy but definitely it is simple'.

'Reconfirm the information'

a very simple and effective solution.

Easy.

No.

How difficult it is to ask everybody to repeat what you have said with an intention of communicating an idea?

But at least we can do so with 'intention transfer':

1. Keep it simple, small and direct.
2. Keep it clear.
3. Reconfirm.
4. Repeat often.

Once the 'intention transfer' is accurate it is easier for the other related communications to be properly understood.

COMMUNICATION - THE ONLY MANAGEMENT TOOL

> *Earlier, I used to think that communication is one of the important tools of a manager.*
>
> *But now I know that communication is the "only" tool available for any management (first level supervisor to the topmost levels).*

Somehow, I am not comfortable with the word manager. We all are in fact 'PROVIDERS'. Our main job is to provide the 5 Ms (men, machines, materials, methods, and/or money) to the 'leaders'. **Leaders who are getting the job done by the 'Doers'.**

The MFH hierarchy is given as -

THE ORGANISATION

DOER

SUPERVISOR

PROVIDER LEVEL 1

PROVIDER LEVEL 2

GUIDE

EXPANDER (The Top Management)

To fulfil this job of, i.e., the providers, guides, and the expanders what do we do?

'We communicate.' Yes.

Anything else, anything more? No.

All hierarchy levels are only doing **'communication'**.

Our only work is -

Communication.

And our only tool is -

Communication.

Now we understand how important it is. For the performance of any individual, any group or any organisation this is the 'only' focus point. Great results or poor results are direct consequences of the quality of communication.

Do we treat this matter with the importance that it should receive?

No, we are busy resolving issues which exist solely because of poor communication.

KEEP YOUR FOCUS ON THE PERFORMERS, ALWAYS

There are three types of team members

First, who do less than what they are supposed to do. They are referred to as *'under-performers'*.

Second, those who do something more than what they are supposed to, the *'over-performers'*.

Third, the most important category are the members who are *'performers'*, who almost always do what they are supposed to do.

Who of the above get the most attention of the management or seniors?

Obviously, the over-performers.

Is it OK?

Who get the most attention of the policy makers?

Obviously, the under-performers.

Is it OK?

Who forms the real organisation?

Yes, the body of the organisation comprises of the 'performers'. They are the people who really drive the organisation forward.

All the policies should be framed to allow and help them to perform rather than trying to force the under-performers into this band. The policies formed for under-performers can be stifling for the performers.

A few over-performers are always good to be there, and they need to be encouraged too. They can be given trophies and awards for appreciation. But the management focus, policies, and systems need to be around the performers.

This subtle change in management focus can be the game changer for the direction and movement of the organisation's future.

NOTHING IS GOOD OR BAD BUT THINKING MAKES IT SO

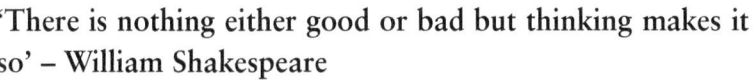

'There is nothing either good or bad but thinking makes it so' – William Shakespeare

These words were used to explain the reality of life. I always hold that business and management are like life. The same words hold very much in the field of management too.

Disclaimer: *this is a made-up example and any resemblance is a coincidence.*

A management system was developed in an organisation, say Japan. It worked very well and gave excellent results. The system was running so well that 'they' decided to reduce their management working hours. The productivity zoomed upwards.

The same was studied by some scholars and they formulated a system based on their studies. This system was implemented in, say 20 organisations in some other country. After a few years it was observed that there were three different results -

1. Derived full benefits and moved in positive direction.
2. At par, no change.
3. Negative impact.

Result: The 'thinking' of the implementers is the key.

The first followed the intention, the thinking of the system, which was aimed at *improving the working condition* of Doers and expediting the decision-making process.

The second took it as a system in *addition to their existing one* and tried to use it as a yardstick to evaluate their existing methods. The results were obvious.

The third went a step further. They started to use it as a *'control tool'*. A totally different perspective and intention. A helping tool was being attempted as a controller owing to the management comfort that the new system promised. Results were obviously...

When adopting a new system, the intention, the thinking of the implementers is to be aligned with the thinking of the developer.

Warning: *intentions have to be monitored at all implementing levels. Any level can distort it and by the time it's diagnosed, it'll be too late.*

THANK YOU

- *To my parents who gave me to the world.*
- *My wife who gave me a re-birth.*
- *My children who guided me during my mental travel from Gen X to Gen Z.*
- *Various organisations where I worked who made me what I am.*
- *To all persons who I met as they all taught me something new every time.*
- *To all writers who shared their experiences and understandings.*
- *Thank you, GOD, (Brahma Vishnu Mahesh...)*